MW01602995

We Look Better Alive

We Look Better Alive

Ali Black

Burnside Review Press   Portland, Oregon

Front Cover Image: Donald Black Jr.,
The Labyrinth, 2010

Cover Design: Susie Steele
Layout: Zach Grow

Printed in the U.S.A.
First Edition, 2025
ISBN: 979-8-9899577-1-2

Burnside Review Press
Portland, Oregon
www.burnsidereview.org

Burnside Review Press titles are available for purchase from the
publisher and Asterism Books (www.asterismbooks.com).

for Emma, Joyce, Gail, Zelma, Alice, and Willie,
the departed matriarchs of my family

the body is the body & inside
there's a person, imagine that? imagine Black
devoid of death, imagine us endless until.

—Danez Smith

COMPLETION

Everyone keeps telling me
my mother looked so pretty
in her casket. They try to assure me
the mortician did a good job.
My mother looked better alive.
She was her prettiest
on holidays. Today at breakfast,
an elder schools me on the beauty
in death. I can listen
for a long time. My grits turn
my catfish soggy. Meanwhile,
she tells me to see death
as a completion, says it's the start
of something new, then tells me
a story about her grandson,
how he looks so much like her son—
same long fingers, dark skin.

The Cost of Beauty (I)

A woman buys a purse
for three thousand dollars
and calls it an investment.
She says Miami is full
of women in wheelchairs
recovering from surgery.
She says some women
never make it home.
After her surgery,
she bloodied up sheet after sheet
then called for her dead mother.
She calls herself lucky
and walks around telling women
to stay away from needles
and knives.

First Funeral in Four Months

I'm a little out of the loop.
Before the service, I buy breath mints
instead of flowers.
I wear the wrong shoes.
I leave my facial tissue in the car.
Inside the chapel, an usher offers me
a seat. I decline and fake like I got it,
like I can stand in Marc Fisher heels
for the full service. My feet burn
during the opening prayer. I no longer
care about bowing my head
and I pray with my eyes open.
I'm trying to say everything
blurs and burns no matter who dies.
Once, my aunt told me she loved
funerals. *I like crying,* she said.
And she has a point.
I see the beauty in people
releasing what's tucked inside.

When My Mother Died

My friends don't come over to help me
sort through my mother's things.
The ashtrays. The bills. The navy blue suits.
No one brings me a home
cooked meal. I don't belong to a church
so there's no pastor stopping by
to read scripture with me.
The neighbor doesn't send her condolences.
The world doesn't stop.
No one grieves the way I do.
I can't find anyone to fry the catfish
the way my mother used to. Hot oil.
Good breading.
I don't ask anyone to pray for me.
The poet says we should grieve
with grace and no one owes you
anything so I walk around
the way my mother used to—
head high, lowkey alone.

What I Want to Say

It's always a woman
asking me when
I'm having a baby.

Today, this one is older—
maybe mid 60s,
a friend of the family.

When we getting a baby?
she asks, as if I owe her.

I wish I could give her
a date, tell her I'm due
in December

then do a little dance.
Instead, I say it's complicated,
do her like my doctor did me—

sit her down, draw her
a picture of my uterus,
circle my ovaries and say

words like *unfortunately*
and *impossible*
and *sorry*.

IMAGINE

my mother alive listening to Meg Thee Stallion

shouting, *real hot girl shit!*

I mean, my mother was a savage.

I've heard the stories about her beating up boys

and dominating on tennis courts.

If my mother was alive,

I'd try to convince her to listen

to Meg. First, I'd play "Body"

and show her all the lyrics.

I'd say, *Ma, Meg celebrates*

our bodies. I'd tell her,

this is how I get my confidence.

And she'd look at me and say,

Now see, for that, I like Meg.

A Friend Wanted to Go Shopping for Bras

and Ma, I took her to Dillard's
because you said the key to buying
a good bra is making the investment
so I warned her and said, *now
Dillard's ain't Target* and I told her
about the sales associates and how they
be tryna make a sale so they greet you fast
and get close and sometimes they touch
your shoulders to adjust the bra straps,
or they touch your back to unhook the bra,
and I told her she gotta let them do their job,
and can you believe she tried to convince
the woman helping us that she was a B cup
but the woman told her she was actually a DD
and she didn't believe the woman until
the woman told her to try the bra on
and once she tried it on and it fit perfectly
she told the woman to bring her the same bra
in every color: mauve, black and beige.

Talkin' to a Friend about Lupus and the Vaccine

Tell your mother to visit the Lupus Foundation's website cuz they talkin'
all about it /sayin' it's still a lot they don't know /talkin' bout we should
work with our doctors and decide if the vaccine is the right thing to do
/ they makin' it seem like this some type of high school science project
/ and see, that's why I got all these questions / like, what if my medicine
don't respond well cuz they already sayin' it's possible that it won't /
and what if I get sick? / and what if it's that off-the-movies type sick
/ that brutal kinda sick / you know what I'm sayin' / and then what?
/ and look at your mom / she had COVID / and she one of the one's
who followed the guidelines / cut herself off from the world like the
world wasn't nothin' but a stubborn gray hair / and can you imagine?
/ your mother a whole ass grown Black woman and she supposed to
listen to somebody tell her what to do / please / but I can't believe she
caught COVID / with lupus / *and* beat it / Damn! / let the church say
hallelujah! / but naw, for real / the pandemic feel like one of them
long long days after someone you love has died / and I felt myself
coming apart like a ripped seam when you said you damn near lost
who you were watchin' your mother's legs swell like a boxer's eye / you
know what I'm sayin' / and trust me / I know what your mother goin'
through / I remember back in 2008 when my legs swelled as if the
whole wide world would burst / they said it was my kidneys / I had a
biopsy and everything / I got a gentle body / I can't be playin' around

KASH DOLL JUST HAD A BABY

She in the gym goin' hard.

Cardio. Weights. You name it.

Don't come for her talkin' about surgery.

Team natural snapback.

No doctors, no knives, no needles.

And like always, y'all in Kash comments wil'n out.

Like, *go burp your baby*, Kash.

Like, *girl, we don't care!*

I say, it's too early for this.

I don't know when I started coming for the comments.

I like it here.

But I only like the users who hype Kash up.

Like, *you go girl.*

Like, *Kash snapback game finna be fire.*

Like, *sis ain't playing no games.*

Like, *Detroit's finest.*

HER BBL

is a case study

a hot song   winner of the P challenge

a distraction

a clapback

a Georgia peach   a manuscript

a weapon

a diss to genetics

not big enough

a showstopper   a threat

a press conference

a performance

we thought we could start a business. We even gave it a name like it was something worth trying. To be fair, the hood was hittin' us up every time a body dropped. This girl wanted a casket wrapped, that dude needed a T-shirt, a bio written, a band booked, a singer scouted, a prayer picked, a balloon released, a flyer posted, the photos gathered, remarks given. I even created a folder and labeled it "Live Forever" and inside that folder I made more folders, labeled each one with a dead person's name. But just like a list, it grew too long and I had to walk away. Funny how death can make you feel invincible. I don't have words these days, but I do have dreams, these ideas that feel urgent and awful all at the same time. Who in their right mind can get to work in times of grief? We thought we could start a business. We even gave it a name.

When My Father-in-Law Died

I read the resolution
and my husband gave the eulogy.
We shot pool at the repast
and took shots of cognac. I thought
about Quan and prayed for death
to let up on us.
For three days straight, people
brought us pans of fried chicken
and sweet Hawaiian rolls.
We never ate any of it.
I thought about asking my grandmother
how to help my grieving husband
and then remembered my grandmother
is gone, so I had to rely on instincts—
cook a meal. Hold him close.

Unofficial Naming Ceremony

I want to remember it a few ways. There was always yellow paper and Milky pens. I wrote every name in cursive but the children I named were never born. I was so brave and ambitious in the 90s. I wanted a son first. I said I'd call him King. I wrote his name so big the yellow paper melted. Sometimes I invited my friends. They brought hot pickles, Faygo and cool ranch Fritos. N always wrote in red. She said it brought her luck. We blushed when we picked out our husbands. We were so pretty and foolish. When I thought of my future daughter I laughed and cried. My mother warned me about revenge and that's when I stopped talking back to her. I told my friends my kids would always wear clean clothes. I promised to be a good mother.

Field Trip: Cleveland, OH

The kids in the afterschool program scream
and run when we walk past an outdoor
art installation full of figurative sculptures
by a Brooklyn-based artist.
They call it a cemetery
and convince each other they see
ghosts. It's logical to fear things
we can't see, our imaginations
dark and dangerous like loaded
guns. A girl sees a purple high-heeled
boot in an empty field and calls it
a kidnapping. Two blocks later, another girl sees
a fence wrapped in yellow caution tape
and calls it a murder.

WE LOOK BETTER ALIVE
On Birthdays, Twerking, and Honoring the Dead

1.

While the birthday girl twerks in the mirror,
her friends record her.
This is the new history. Hands up. Cameras out.
The DJ plays Trap Beckham's "Birthday Bitch"
and shouts out all the Virgos. The birthday girl
bends over and her friends slap her butt.
She gives a wild and passionate twerk.
The men, staring from a distance, bob their heads
to the beat and smile. Four bottle service girls
bring bottles of champagne topped with sparklers
and a sign that reads, "One time for the birthday girl!"
Everything is so turnt I forget
this city is the worst place
for Black women to be alive.

2.

For Black women to be alive.
This is what I wish for every morning
when I wake up to check my city's news
page on Instagram. Almost every morning,
I read about another dead Black woman.

Last night, I made it home safe.

Last night, the birthday girl twerked
for two songs straight. Last night, a local
celebrity made it home safe, then she was killed.

Now her story is all over Instagram.
Somebody is in the comments saying
it was a domestic dispute and suggests we
keep our comments to ourselves
because we don't know the full story.

3.

Because we don't know the full story,

the birthday girl begs for white roses.

I guess this is what people mean

when they say, give me my flowers

while I'm still alive. At the bar,

I give the birthday girl a small bouquet

of white roses. She sets them down

and takes a video of the scene—

the flowers, her glass of peach Bellini,

her sequined clutch purse.

This is her history.

We are so blessed to be alive

in my city. Every other day,

another Black woman dies.

4.

Another Black woman dies

and I've made it my job to write about them.

When I was younger, the funerals I attended

only had Black women in the caskets.

My aunt was buried wearing her white

wedding dress. There was so much mud

at her burial we ruined our shoes.

I can't remember my great-grandmother's funeral.

I've lost too many of my favorite women.

Back then, I didn't know words

could keep Black women alive.

Last week, a woman holding a baby

was shot and killed in a front yard.

My city has so much work to do.

5.

My city has so much work to do
to keep Black women out of caskets.
It takes a Bloomberg report to say
Cleveland is the worst city for Black women
before the Mayor pretends to pay attention.
He tries to start a commission
for Black women and girls. He fails.
I don't believe in mayors
who are silent whenever a Black woman dies.
The Mayor owes us an apology.
I mean, yesterday the birthday girl told me
she lost her grandmother, said
they found her dead in her home.
She'd been dead for days.

6.

She'd been dead. For days,
I couldn't stop thinking
about the birthday girl
and her late grandmother.
For days, the birthday girl searched
through her grandmother's old things.
She found a pair of vintage Louis Vuitton loafers.
They'd be cute on you, she said.
But I've never worn a dead woman's shoes.
Maybe that's how I should honor the dead.
For days, the birthday girl danced in the mirror.
For days, the birthday girl ate expensive meals.
Maybe this is how
she honors the dead.

7.

She honors the dead
by celebrating her birthday for six days straight.
All this celebrating, all this twerking,
all these flowers, all those caskets
for Black women.
Today we twerk.
Today we toast.
Today we take the birthday girl out
to celebrate while another Black woman
is killed. I am always thinking about Black women
dying. This is a way to honor the dead.
Tonight, I honor the dead
by asking the DJ to cut the music
while the birthday girl twerks in the mirror.

On Visiting Aunt Rosa & Car Racing

Looking just like your mother,
my Aunt says when she sees me
and I wonder how she does it.
You know, look at me,
see her sister
(who was once here
all alive, gap-toothed
and long-legged),
and still invite me in her home.
I don't know if I could
face the face of my dead sister.
Today, I'm here for my mother's
stories. The ones she took
with her when she left.
I want my Aunt to tell me
about my mother's modeling days
and how she learned to cook
and when she learned to braid
and who taught her how to swing
a bat, her hips, a tennis racket.
We drink sweet tea and munch
on roasted cashews.
My Aunt tells me about her days
in the Powder Puff
and how she loved racing cars
and how my mother loved
to *see them cars go!*

LAB RESULTS

I call the doctor back
to go over my labs.

He leads with,
this is not the news

any of us expected.
He rambles off numbers

I don't completely understand.
But I know when somebody is breaking

my heart. A poet wonders
if she's supposed to carry grief

instead of children. I wonder
if I'm supposed to raise

other people's children
since I'll never have my own.

Rihanna & A$AP Rocky Stroll a Harlem Street

This is not a drill. You change the history of the pregnancy photoshoot because you decided to wear a hot-pink vintage Chanel puffer coat with jeweled gold buttons? You're such an icon. Your post gets close to twenty million likes and the people go in in the comments. They call you pretty and claim you as they baby mama. They hope you have a girl. They send prayers up. They heart-eye-emoji-you. They ask, *where the album at?* They swear you havin' twins. The haters say you ain't the first pregnant woman in the world. They insert the throw-up emoji, give you a thumbs down, call you a narcissist. You give em' more legs, more heels, more skin.

STRETCH MARKS

First, know this:
when the inflammation of lupus
attacks the kidneys, fluid builds
in the body and the doctors give it
a name. They say *edema,* but I just say
swelling. Either way, it appears in your feet,
legs, ankles, eyelids, and sometimes your entire body,
which can be a sign of something serious.
The doctors call this *lupus nephritis,*
but I just say potential
kidney failure. And yeah,
this was my story back in '08,
but here's what you don't know:
when my body began to swell—
like can't-fit-my-shoes swell,
like I-needed-a-kidney-biopsy swell,
like life-or-death swell—
all I worried about was getting stretch marks.
Every night, I had a thousand
questions for my nurse.
Will the stretch marks be dark?
Will they come on my arms?
What about my breasts?
I had the nurse rubbing Vaseline
all over my stomach thinking I could
outsmart the universe's plan.
But, the stretch marks were victorious,
like a toddler scribbling lines.
Never once did I ask the nurse anything
about dying.

SELF-PORTRAIT AS THE PRETTY GIRL

After one more person tells me
I look pretty, I reach in my purse
for my compact mirror.
I gotta see for myself.
I reapply my light rose
lip-gloss by Chanel.
I don't have the prettiest
smile but it's alright for a girl
with two pegged teeth.
My mama covered them with dental
crowns before I went to college.
She said they'd give me confidence.
People don't know this
but I used to pray for bigger
lips. When they be callin' me pretty
I be thinkin' about Whitney.
I'd do almost anything
for Rihanna's smile, her Cupid's bow.
I wonder what my life would be
like if I woulda had bigger lips.
The worst thing about it is
I can't find whose lips I have.
I've studied the faces
of everyone in my family,
still haven't seen mine anywhere.

Draya sells   swimwear. Draya is a model. Draya spreads   her legs.
Draya wears green. Draya raises her arms. Draya hides   her eyes.
Draya stirs   the net. *Draya, close   your legs.* Draya never replies.
Draya has long feet. Draya is fire. Draya makes them   drool. Draya
is wide   open. Draya is unbothered. Draya is not   on her way.
Draya wants   love. Draya keeps the photo. Draya is naughty.
Draya is the perfect angle. Draya gets hella likes. Draya makes money.
Draya is body goals. Draya is ice cold.

What My Girls Say When I Ask If They Would Ever Get a BBL

Absolutely not. You couldn't pay me to fly down south to wake up
in a recovery room
alone and slumped over in a cold steel wheelchair like somebody
sick auntie.

I would if I had the money and the surgeon could promise I
wouldn't die.
In other words, run me the best surgeon, the ones with waitlists.

Never. I know this girl who had one and her surgeon did a good job
but homegirl said she wouldn't wish the recovery process on her
worst enemy.

Sign me up for a hot girl summer and give me a nice juicy peach!
Might get me one next winter so I can be a baddie come June.

Look at K. Michelle. She started having pain in her back and legs,
said it was one of the worst decisions of her life.

I think they look good on some girls. I'd have to do my research,
ask the baddest bitch in the club, see what she say.

Hell to the no. Them chicks look crazy. Body all lopsided and
disproportioned. I'd rather
work out. Do some stairs. Go heavy on the squats. Pay for a trainer.
Not the knife.

How to Steam a Polyester Dress

Sometimes I forget who I am
and do things my mother would be ashamed of.
Like I haven't watered my plants in weeks,
I see smudges on my mirror, and the travel sized
toothpaste is still in my suitcase.

Once, I ordered a dress online
and spent two days googling "dry cleaners
near me." It's like I'm addicted to convenience,
but I'm also good at pretending
I can't do something.

I *know* I can iron the dress
and yet, I still go to YouTube and search
"how to steam a polyester dress"
as if I don't come from Zelma
and Alice and Emma.

I don't need to google anything.
All I need is my memory so I think back
to my mother in our basement ironing,
and remember I need the hot water,
the starch, and that cream pressing cloth.

THE COST OF BEAUTY (II)

The woman I know who knows the woman who died
from a tummy tuck never talks about it. I want to ask
the woman who knows the woman who died from a tummy tuck
if they ever talked about their bodies
but another woman's body ain't none of my business.

When My Grandmother Died

I want all my people alive
and yet, my grandmother dies
in her daughter's house.
Three of my grandmother's daughters
couldn't be there for her death.
They were already gone.
My grandmother buried three of her daughters
and no one said a word
about what it did to her. My point is—
silence is grief's favorite weapon
and I've watched it destroy family
after family. My family is lost without the women
who left us. When my grandmother died, I heard her
last breath. I thought back to the 80s and all
the time we spent at her house playing Pokeno
and dancing to Michael and eating
her peach cobbler. Now, my family is lost
in the silence.

WHEN RALPH DIED

I was sitting in a gallery
waiting for a poetry reading
to start and somebody posted
RIP Ralph on Facebook.
Sometimes I mistake social
media for a monster.
Sometimes I'm right.
It's a scary thing to open an app
and find out your childhood friend
has died. When Ralph died, I flashed
back to basketball, to his three-pointer,
to streetlights, to bike rides, to Willo,
to Euclid, to front porches, to backyards,
to radio, to jokes, to his mother.

Oh my God,
his mother.

ANOTHER SCHOOL SHOOTING

Outside the school, the school boy asks
if I've heard about the children
in Texas who were murdered.
He looks up to the flag, which was missing
all school year, and points. *Look, they forgot
to raise it to the top,* he says.
I tell him, the flag is at half-staff
to honor the children who died.
I offer him a Starburst to interrupt
the silence. He declines the pink juicy
chew. I forget this is the boy who lowered
his head and offered a moment of silence
when I told him my Akita killed
a skunk in our backyard. For weeks,
my bookbag smelled like the skunk
and for weeks the school boy kept asking,
did you wash your bookbag,
did you wash it yet? I'm starting to think
he wasn't worried about my bag.
He was worried about the smell
of death, how it lingers.
How it spreads.

SELF-PORTRAIT AS A GROWN WOMAN

I almost spill my wine when a friend
tells me I got "grown woman" beauty.
I don't see myself as grown—I laugh
during professional development.
I keep Gen Zers close. They teach me
the renegade and keep me up
to speed. A magazine says
there are eleven beauty lessons
every grown woman should know.
#7 tells you to get your brows done—
further proof I don't meet the standards.

Thoughts at the Funeral

I don't completely agree with the pastor
when he says today is a celebration.

Funerals don't come with joy,
not for me anyway. The flowers

arranged around the casket make me sad.
We say, *give people their flowers*

while they're alive, so now these flowers feel
out of place, like, too little, too late.

The two-minute remarks make me sad.
No one is prepared. The pastor's eulogy

feels a little, *I didn't do my homework*
so let me lean on Jesus. And this is why

my brother always says he don't want no pastor
talkin' over his body like that. We mumble

the Lord's prayer and I think back to high school
when we used to recite this same prayer

before every track meet. Now I say *forever*
and forget to say *Amen.*

Wet Ass Pu**y

I know some of y'all don't care for the Cardi B's out there cuz y'all think the music too raunchy. I read y'all complaints to the FCC when Cardi & Meg performed "WAP" on the Grammys. Said they were disgusting, that they were sluts being sluts. Said y'all felt violated and your children couldn't sleep. Said you wanted to seek legal action. Said their performance was trash, obscene. But I like the way the music makes me feel—all sexy, all woman, all human. Even Nicki. Every time I hear her say, *big titties, big butt too,* I hold my head higher.

a girl gives me props and calls me a strong force. I think she was really tryna say she can't believe I don't be trippin over my man takin pictures of a nude woman. She right but she don't know the whole story. It ain't always been like this, meaning, I ain't always been good with my husband takin photos of nude women. But the crazy thing about it is I don't know why. It ain't like I didn't use to see my mother naked every time she got out the tub and walked from the bathroom to her bedroom. She never wore a towel. Then she would sit on the edge of her bed, prop her small vanity mirror on her purse and put her makeup on. *Naked as a jaybird,* as she used to say. I used to bring her tissue, cotton balls, Vaseline, whatever she needed. I never felt no kind of way about her naked body. It was what it was. She was my mother. Her body had that kind of power. She could do what she wanted with it. But then we started learnin that a naked body was a bad thing and by the time I got to middle school and had to take showers after swim class, the only people walking around naked were the white girls. We thought they were so reckless. You couldn't catch us walkin around without a towel. We were learnin that our naked bodies were for private. Same thing in college. We used to be disgusted by all them white girls walking around naked in the locker room. VP used to act like she was about to earl every time she saw one. We would die laughin. But ain't nobody wanna see all that. And them white girls ain't give a damn. I think the Hip Hop had a lot to do with us thinkin a naked Black woman was a sin. Men be actin like our bodies are meant for them. Like, I used to date a few men who had hella insecurity issues so they always had somethin to say about how I dressed if I ever put on something short or tight. All this twisted my mind up so by the time I'm thirty and I meet my husband and he takin pictures of nude women, I'm like aw hell naw! I don't trust that shit. I used to think a man lookin at a naked woman through a camera automatically meant it's gone lead to sex. It meant this dude might risk it all, meant somebody about to cheat. And then, the more I started to get to know my husband and I saw that he was a different type of dude, a man who ain't swayed by a naked body, a man who at the shoot really tryna make art, I started losin trust in the women! I was like, well, my issue ain't with my husband, it's with these chicks and I don't trust none of em'. I got a good dude. These chicks uh do anything to get a dude like him. I remember this one time he showed me some photos from a shoot he did and I couldn't take it. I had to excuse myself. I went to the bathroom and got sick to my stomach. I was cryin about the shit. I ain't gone lie, this almost fucked up our relationship. I was lettin my imagination twist reality. It was bad. I had to talk to my elders about it—my Aunt and CP, this old Black photographer who's a good friend of ours. My Aunt was basically tellin me I had to change my thinkin, like, girl grow up, stop bein so immature about it. CP told me to look up a Black photographer who was famous for takin pictures of nude Black women. I can't remember that photographer's name but I remember CP just breakin down the art in nudity. After a while, I'm like, *oh wow—I'm trippin.* I'm the one on some bullshit. And the worst part about it is that my own shit was affectin my husband on an artistic level, like I was reckin his flow like Lisa in *Love Jones.* He stopped shootin nudes because of me and I ain't like that. I realized I was bein reckless. I had to let all that go. So when the girl called me a strong force, all I could think about was how long it took me to be one.

How to Wash a Bra

I never wash my bras
on the delicate cycle.
I never wash them by hand,
placing them in the sink
to soak like collard greens.
They never air-dry or hang
on a line. I never take my time
to fasten the hooks.
I don't go by the books.
I wash my bras on normal—
a subtle act of harm.
When I take them out the dryer
I cuss at the snags. I'm mad
at the lace. My bras deserve more.
They keep important things in place.

LITTLE BLACK DRESS

I bought that little black dress I saw on Emprada and thought it was kinda made for me—short, black, ruched, burnout mesh. I say kinda because it was one of those one shoulder dresses and all my girls D cups and bigger know what I mean by this. I'm talking strapless bra. Strapless as in: So hard to find. Strapless as in: Not enough support. Strapless as in: A good one gone cost you at least a benny a.k.a. a hundred dollars—I learned that from the music. Strapless as in: Insecure. Strapless as in: Maybe I shouldn't buy the dress in the first place. Strapless as in: I read all of the reviews and even that's a risk, cuz I only trust the girls who post pics. Strapless as in: Tape is not an option. Strapless as in: Buy the dress and the bra and practice moving around at home. Strapless as in: Leave all the tags on.

Dress Code for the Women's Luncheon

When we walked into the fancy hall
T   dressed in a pink and black spaghetti-strapped dress
used her arms to make an X across her body
to cover her chest   or maybe it was her heart
either way   I was there   trying
to convince her to forget   everything
she's ever learned about a dress   code
and how it tries to   control who   belongs
where   based on who wears   what
I told her   we are special   guests
and still   she never took her arms down

Confidence Workshop

My job description says I'm required
to boost self-esteem and confidence
in girls. So when I watch
the coolest girl shrink to a small
knot when it's her turn to come up front
and say her name to the group, I cut
the lesson short. I don't like to confuse learning
with agony, so we stop and sit
in a small circle to hold hands like family.
When we let go of each other,
I make a list of all my insecurities
and write them on the board
with a marker. I choose red.

DaniLeigh had a baby. DaniLeigh looks   good. DaniLeigh snapped back. DaniLeigh is pressure. DaniLeigh has money. DaniLeigh feels good. DaniLeigh throws up   the peace sign. DaniLeigh dances. DaniLeigh has a flat   stomach. DaniLeigh didn't gain weight. DaniLeigh is in shape. DaniLeigh looks   confident. DaniLeigh is DaniLeigh. DaniLeigh isn't   responsible. DaniLeigh doesn't care. DaniLeigh minds her business. DaniLeigh shares   her business. DaniLeigh's body is inspiration. DaniLeigh is young. DaniLeigh only has one child. DaniLeigh dates a rapper.

My Students Ask Why I Don't Have Any Children

I sing them a song until they fall asleep. It's a snowy Monday and we don't have time for the honest to god truth. Sometimes I can never find the words. How do you say complicated in slang? I avoid the question the same way I avoid the doctor who wants me to believe everything he says. It'll take me years to explain how disappointing science can be. When the kids wake up, I feed them cold ham and watch them drink white milk. I peel an orange for the smallest girl. She shows me her best wink. It's better than yesterday's. Yes, I've been teaching her how to fly.

AFTER-VISIT SUMMARY

Date: March 13, 2021

Doctor: Dr. Ryan X. Kaufman

Impression: 40 year old Black female, interested in using a gestational surrogate due to hx of lupus and Cellcept

Topics discussed:

1) Reviewed process, estimated costs, impact of her age on egg quality/quantity

2) Recommended search agencies—Compassionate Beginnings—to select surrogate

3) Will do prelim labs, see again to review and refer for IVF

Plan: See above, needs SA, AMH and preconception labs and sonography for ovary accessibility

Provided patient information packets: infertility, IVF—card for IVF program

Total time spent dedicated to this encounter: Approximately 30 minutes

The Cost of Beauty (III)

I know a woman who knows
a woman who died.
The woman who died
wanted a new body.
She flew out of the country
to buy one.
I don't have too many
more details.
What I know is enough.
And there's this:
The woman who died
has a daughter. A daughter
who already wants
a new body.
Smaller breasts,
a bigger butt.

On Infertility

My students wish me
a Happy Mother's Day.
I don't tell them how much
it hurts. They bring me my favorite
things. Hot popcorn. Moleskin
journals. Sharpie pens. I picture the children
I will never have. Black babies
with heads full of hair. I don't want
to sound ungrateful. I just like telling
the truth. Today a teen boy
tells me I'd be a good mother.
He says, *so when you gone*
have some kids? It comes out like
a plea rather than a question.

Beyoncé stands on hay. Beyoncé wears a cowboy hat. Beyoncé looks back
at   the camera. Beyoncé shows her   peach. Beyoncé doesn't blink.
Beyoncé is a cowgirl. Beyoncé is above this. Beyoncé doesn't ask why.
Beyoncé ain't mad. Beyoncé understood the assignment. Beyoncé's
peach is   a bubble. Beyoncé could have kept this. Beyoncé is a
mother. Beyoncé can pose. Beyoncé breaks her rule. Beyoncé doesn't
have to   do this. Beyoncé is comfortable. Beyoncé looks good.
Beyoncé is an   example. Beyoncé wears blue. Beyoncé is past this.
Beyoncé doesn't tag   the doctor. Beyoncé works out. Beyoncé is a
bucket list. Beyoncé is natural. Beyoncé isn't disappointed. Beyoncé
is   grown.

FREAKNIK

I swear you tell the best stories.
Remember when you told me
about the first time you went
to Freaknik? Not the big one
in Atlanta, but you said
they had one in Cleveland at Woodhill.
You said there was a girl wearing
a bikini and she was dancing
on top of a car shaking her ass,
then a dude pulled her
down and dudes got to ripping
her clothes off and then twelve came
and the officer literally carried the girl
out the park and I was in disbelief
while you telling the story
I asked, *you were there?*
and you were like, *Yeah. I was there*
and the cop was running outta the park
with this naked woman on his back.

When Quan Died

This might sound weird
but—hands down—Quan
had the rawest homegoing.
D Black made this mosaic image
of Quan's face and put it on a shirt
and the whole hood lined up
outside our garage to buy one to rock
to the funeral. We made so many
the printer broke and that was my proof
that Quan was the type of dude that would
make an impact on everything forever.
When the pastor invited the family
to the casket for a final viewing,
I swear to God a vase shattered
and the flowers fell to the floor.
And when the funeral was over,
D Black rode his Ripper to the gravesite
popping wheelies all up and down Kinsman.
At 144th, we all blew our horns
cuz that was Quan's street
and Shalon and them was hanging
out the car windows dancing as they blasted
Quan's song. But the best thing
was when Alvin started doing backflips
at the cemetery. I got chills watching him
cuz I know how death can make you
want to wreck some shit, but your body
won't let you so you do whatever else
comes out. We kicked it at the repast.
We played Quan's song and did his dance

and sipped our drinks
to celebrate and numb ourselves.

Shots Fired on New Year's Eve

My auntie always hid in the front closet whenever they started shooting. That same closet stored my grandfather's shotgun, so I never understood why any of us were ever afraid. We could shoot back. This New Year's Eve my brother had his pistol and my friend fired the whole clip. Every loved one we know in heaven smiled. I held my breath and when it was over I mistook the drywall dust from our walls for gun powder—it covered my friend's shoulder. We were dressed in black and took shots of cognac. We danced to Future. When the ball dropped, I forgot to give my annual kiss. If I could relive the night, I'd fire the gun into the big black sky.

We drive into Athens blasting Kendrick.
D Black lowers the volume and brags

about Kendrick's courage, says,
niggas ain't ready for real artistic expression.

D Black's voice is so alive
I mistake it for the song's bass.

We got the beast in the back.
She lifts up, excited by all the male

vibrations. I expect her to bark,
but she keeps it cool and listens

like a good girl. We near the exit.
At D Black's request, I hit

record to capture the Ohio University sign.
We pass the college dorms and I mistake them

for the projects—so slim, so tall,
so brown. The dorms and stadiums trigger

D Black, and, like Kendrick, he spits
out story after story of all his college days.

He's talking Black men, white town.
I get anxious. I take note of how many times

he says *police, arrest,* and *murder.*
I know his characters all too well.

I can swap their names with friends
I once knew: The guy who gets murdered,

the girl who gets pregnant. He talks white boys,
beer, and dudes getting smacked

with bottles. Our first stop is Siegfried,
the college hall for visual artists.

I take Kodie, the beast, while D Black goes
inside to make the past and present meet.

Kodie barks at two white kids
carrying neon poster boards.

Her bark makes me feel important
more than it makes me feel protected.

*

We meet J, D Black's homie from college,
and head towards the North End.

At the North End, we order a round
and our waitress gives Kodie a small bowl of water.

All the patrons want to engage with Kodie.
It's the first time white folks have disturbed us

without anything turning deadly. I am so proud
of Kodie. We are the most beautiful things

at the restaurant. D Black and J reminisce.
I call their college town dangerous,

a landscape set up to harm Black men.
J talks violence and D Black remembers

the time *a nigga pulled a gun out* on him.
This is what I mean by feeling anxious.

I thank god for Kodie. She distracts me
from the two men I love talking death,

trauma and baby mamas. They school me
on conflict, how to distinguish the weak

from the naïve, thug from the fool.
A slurred white girl wants to know if she can

pet Kodie. D Black tells her no,
explains Kodie is having culture shock.

The white girl nods and walks away.
I laugh inside and sip my apple whiskey.

Two Weeks after Ralph Died

I guess we deserve to drink like this?
Red cups, brown liquor.

Cheers on three.

My friends are dyin' and we just keep toastin'
like there's really somethin' to celebrate.

Shit don't be addin' up.
Today, our twenty year high school reunion.

Yesterday, Ralph's funeral.
We way too young to be buryin' each other.

At the reunion, I don't know what to say
to the white girl I don't recognize when she asks me,

Do you remember me?
Of course I don't.

We just buried my friend.
My homie from preschool.

The first guy who crushed on me.
The boy with all the J's.

The only kid on the street
with a real hoop in his backyard.

The classmate with good jokes,
the kind that cracked us up.

I never even had a chance
to toast with Ralph.

I'm sick of toastin'
to my friends who can't toast back.

My Brother Grieves

I did a search on my phone to see how many times you've sent me songs to listen to on TIDAL. The messages go back to 2017. It's been five years and I still haven't downloaded TIDAL so every time you send me a song I have to look it up on Apple Music. I can't just click on your message. I have to remember the name of the song and type it into Apple Music's search. It's a process. I'm not complaining. I just wanted you to know. I'll be honest though. I haven't listened to every song you've sent—especially the ones post February 2021. Sometimes I forget. Sometimes I try to forget. This morning, I listened to that song you sent me by Dax, "Dear Alcohol." I couldn't finish it. I kept hearing you say, *this song is exactly how I feel,* and I don't know if I'm ready to know exactly how you feel. It's a lot. I'm sorry I keep replying to your messages with songs I think you should listen to. I really thought "Hero" by Mariah Carey was a good response to that song you sent me about love and regret. You never responded. How should I respond to those songs you send me? Do you want a response or do you just want me to listen? I have a hard time grieving collectively. I don't like seeing other people sad. I suppress a lot. My love keeps telling me to make a list of things I don't talk about. I keep making the list and losing it.

GOING TO EUCLID

I grew up with a lot of white people.
The white girls I played soccer with ate
boxed Kraft macaroni and cheese
as a snack. They cooked their hotdogs
in the microwave and feathered
their blonde bangs with L'Oréal hairspray.
They cheated on tests and never
got caught. In high school, my teacher mocked
my last name. *McClain complain. McClain
complain.* Some white people tell a lot of lies.
My brother has more proof
than I do. Back then, our parents stayed
talking to our coaches. I saw my mother
walk up to one with a note pad to document
his bullshit. He used to bench our star Black players
so second-string white boys could play.
One time, I took my jersey off
after a big loss and my coach
looked at me like I had plans to set the field
on fire in my sports bra. Another time,
me and my crew got suspended
for wearing khaki pants with light denim shirts.
The principal called it gang behavior.

Lizzo Makes a Music Video

Lizzo is out the house. Lizzo wears gold. Lizzo is a goddess. Lizzo has haters. Lizzo likes to twerk. Lizzo cries. Lizzo wears sheer. Lizzo is a rumor. Lizzo plays the flute. Lizzo sings with Cardi. Lizzo licks her lips. Lizzo gets hella views. Lizzo is "inappropriate." Lizzo is smiling. Lizzo plays on repeat. Lizzo smacks her teeth. Lizzo is a masterpiece. Lizzo deserves an Oscar. Lizzo makes it look easy. Lizzo gets cancelled. Lizzo cuts them loose. Lizzo walks slow. Lizzo stuns the world.

THE CUSTOM CASKET

Quan left the earth ten days ago
and now D Black has to wrap the casket.

What a life. The man can do
anything. Today, it's adhering a vinyl print

to the white metal casket.
I watch him work.

He has printed the design,
gathered his tools—a silver box cutter,

a small blue squeegee. He sits on
a Lowe's bucket, his body eye-level

to the casket. It's a sad scene—
our garage, the place where we make

things for the dead. Poems, prints,
and now custom caskets.

AUNT ROSA MAKES A PHOTO COLLAGE OF HER & ALL HER SISTERS
after Brittany Rogers, and in memory of my mother, Aunt Joyce, and Aunt Gail

In this collage,   they sharp.

Aunt Joyce with the red suit   thin white trim on the collar
        buttons so clean I could cry
She look so good alive   teeth just as bright
and straight   gold chain glowing on her golden skin

My mother: Zelma   bottom left, two-piece gray suit
with the white V-neck blouse   loose Anita Baker curls
chunky gold earrings   cheekbones high as heaven
something in the distance glistens   She look so good alive

Aunt Gail shines in the center   scarlet lip
white mink jacket   just above the knee
this the Aunt Gail after the golden blonde hair
I see you Auntie   with that flawless Johnson girl skin
She look so good alive   eyeliner so perfect her eyes purr

Right above, Aunt Rosa in a blue blazer   bronze lip
Two loose black curls frame her forehead
She look so good alive   the bush behind her content
with the way she takes up space   gleaming with grace

To the right of her   Aunt Diane   she so fine
the collage could collapse   dressed in all black
sweet strawberry lip   with the low pixie cut
She look so good alive
I see diamonds on her jacket   praise for good lighting

Far left, Aunt Gene   my queen of Detroit

Stone colored trench   sea blue shirt underneath
              got the gold body curls
She look so good alive   wearing a rouge red lip
       my girl fine as they come

Aunt Crystal, bottom right   baby sis   laughing like always
gap tooth   low fade   navy tee
all the joy you can see   She look so good alive

NOVEMBER'S GRIEF

Regina King says, *grief is love that has no place to go.*
I type the quote in my Notes then open Twitter.

Questlove tweets about Takeoff.
Migos flood my timeline. Every time someone dies,

I lose my appetite then braid my hair.
Grief makes me crave convenience.

November just started and the kids keep posting,
"Long Live" so-and-so. Before dusk, they release balloons

into a sky that never responds. I'm getting bored
with how we grieve—all the red cups, all the brown

liquor, all the skunk-smelling smoke.
When I'm gone, please sober up.

NOTES

The epigraph for the book is from Danez Smith's poem "alive" from *Bluff* (Graywolf Press).

"Aunt Rosa Makes a Photo Collage of Her & All Her Sisters" is written after Brittany Rogers' poem "Ode to My Mama and 'The Purple Dress,' Circa 1992 – 1993" from *Good Dress* (Tin House Books).

ACKNOWLEDGMENTS

Many thanks to the following journals in which these poems,
sometimes in different versions, originally appeared:

The Adroit Journal: "Once Everybody Started Dying," "Stretch
Marks," and "The Custom Casket"

Cleveland Review of Books: "First Funeral in Four Months" and "On
Visiting Aunt Rosa & Car Racing"

Gulf Coast: "When My Mother Died" and "Going to Euclid"

Live Encounters: "What I Want to Say"

Muzzle Magazine: "We Look Better Alive"

swamp pink: "When Quan Died"

I often talk about how I don't have a writing community. I need to stop
talking like that. Thank you to all the people who support my work.

To Dan Kaplan and the staff at Burnside Review Press, many
thanks for pouring into this book.

I wrote a lot of these poems to honor and celebrate Black
women. Shout out to us! To my cousin Kim, aunts, friends, and
celebrities mentioned—I thank y'all for inspiring me.

Special thank you to Mary Biddinger, Hilary Plum, Caryl Pagel,
and Taylor Byas for helping edit early versions of these poems. I
am grateful for your wisdom and time.

Thank you to Aracelis Girmay and Taylor Byas for writing blurbs for this book. My deepest appreciation to you both.

Thank you to Na-Te' Sturdivant. The title poem of this book is inspired by you. You truly mean the world to me and my work.

Finally, thank you to my love, Donald Black Jr. These poems weren't easy to write. Grief floods this book and this life. To help with the healing, your go-to advice for me is always this: "Write about it." I am forever grateful for you.

Ali Black is a writer from Cleveland, Ohio. She is the author of *We Look Better Alive* (Burnside Review Press, 2025) and *If It Heals at All* (Jacar Press, 2020), which was selected by Jaki Shelton Green for the New Voices Series and named a finalist for the 2021 Ohioana Book Award in Poetry. Her writing has appeared in *The Offing, jubilat, Literary Hub, Muzzle Magazine, The Adroit Journal,* and elsewhere. She is the co-founder of Balance Point Studios, a nonprofit organization dedicated to making, teaching, and sharing art.

"'Back then, I didn't know words / could keep Black women alive.' Alive talking to the dead across the threshold of death. Alive under lights and music. Alive with words in her mouth and hand. Ali Black writes right into deep zones of feeling. Havoc, sorrow, isolation, togetherness, desire—often all at once. Line after line an assertion of breath carrying its range of memories, details, and astonishments, like: 'She look so good alive / the bush behind her...' Black's words blessing the living with all that daring, honest looking. And blessing the dead, keeping them alive by the utter force of her attention."

—Aracelis Girmay

"What really fascinates me about Ali Black's *We Look Better Alive* is how it complicates our understanding of dying. There are literal deaths scattered throughout the book: funerals for a mother, for a father-in-law, reports of a grandmother's passing, a friend's. And yet this collection seems most concerned about the metaphorical deaths Black women experience in their quest for beauty and acceptance. From doctor's offices, to school classrooms, and even to the social media pages of female celebrities, Black leads us through a museum of death, demonstrates how society robs Black women of life at every turn."

—Taylor Byas